A FIRST LOOK AT INSECTS

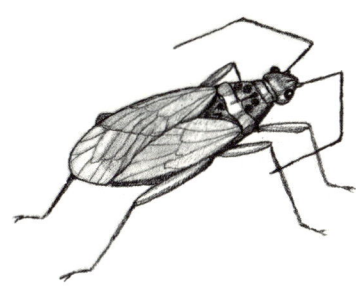
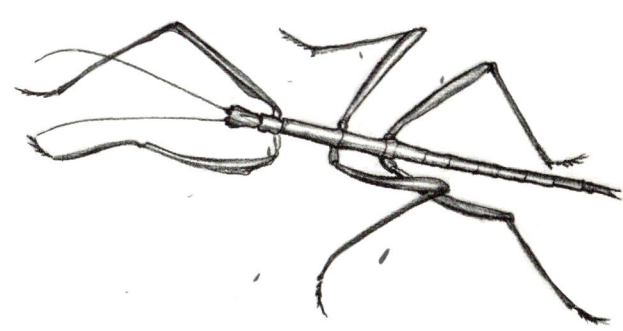

By Millicent E. Selsam and Joyce Hunt

ILLUSTRATED BY HARRIETT SPRINGER

WALKER AND COMPANY · NEW YORK

For
Jonas and Pearl

The authors wish to thank
John C. Pallister, Research Assistant
in the Department of Entymology
at the American Museum of Natural
History, for reading the text of this book.

Text copyright © 1974 by Millicent E. Selsam and Joyce Hunt
Illustrations copyright © 1974 by Harriett Springer
All rights reserved.
No part of this book may
be reproduced or transmitted in any form or by
any means, electronic or mechanical, including
photocopying, recording, or by any information
storage and retrieval system, without permission
in writing from the Publisher.

First published in the United States of America
in 1974 by the Walker Publishing Company, Inc.

Published simultaneously in Canada by
Fitzhenry & Whiteside, Limited, Toronto.

Trade ISBN: 0-8027-6181-X
Reinf ISBN: 0-8027-6182-8

Library of Congress Catalog Card Number: 73-92451

Printed in the United States of America

10 9 8 7 6 5 4 3 2 1

A *FIRST LOOK AT* SERIES

Each of the nature books
for this series is planned to develop
the child's powers of observation
and give him or her a rudimentary grasp
of scientific classification.

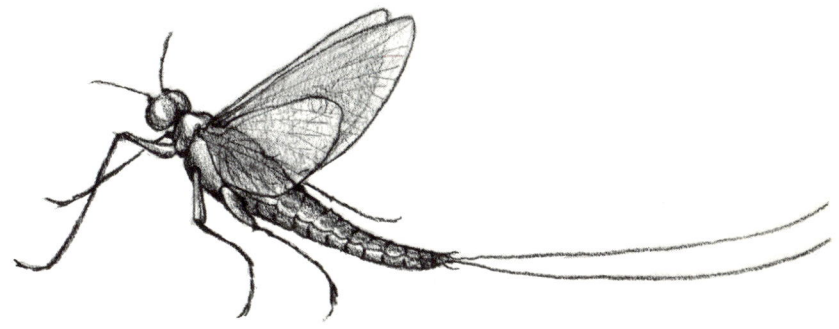

Insects are animals that have a hard covering
on the outside of their bodies.
It is a kind of skeleton
that protects the soft insides.

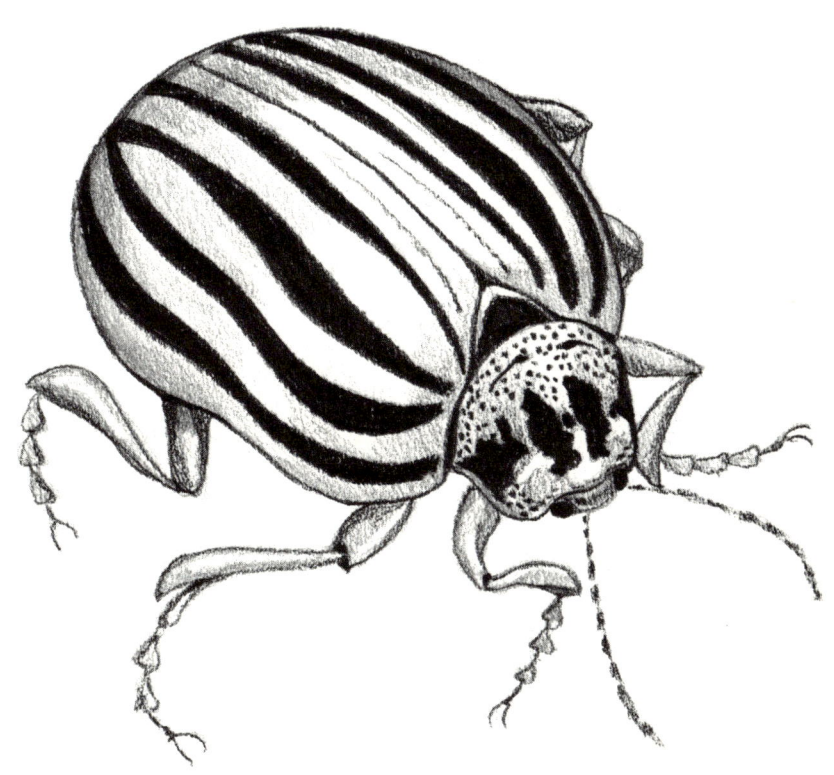

This is an animal that has
its skeleton on the outside.

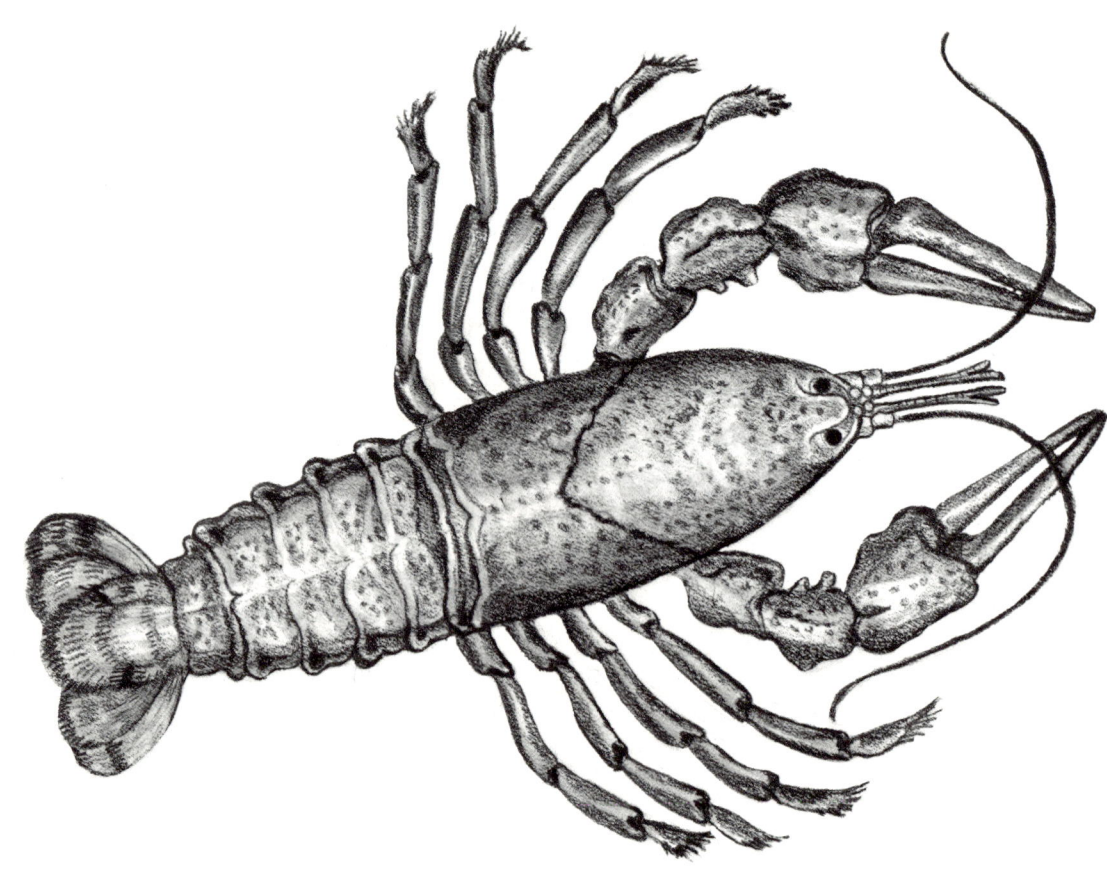

Is it an insect?
No, it is a lobster.

This is another animal that has
its skeleton on the outside.

Is it an insect?
No, it is a spider.

This is still another animal that has an outside skeleton.

Is it an insect?
No, it is a centipede.

Here is one more animal that has an outside skeleton.
But it is an insect.
*It is an insect because it also has six legs
and its body is divided into three parts.
The three parts are called the head, thorax, and abdomen.*

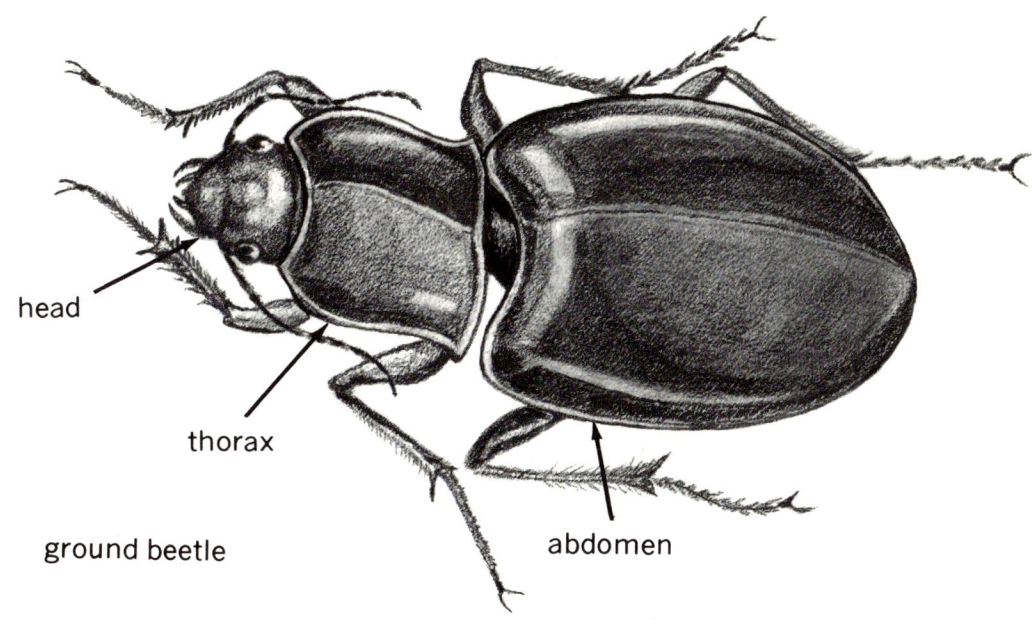

ground beetle

Now go back and count the legs
of the lobster, the spider, and the centipede.

Do they have six legs?

Are their bodies divided into three parts?

Are they insects?

How can you tell one insect from another?
Sometimes you can tell by its shape.

Find the insect that looks like a nail with wings.

Find the insect that looks like a pineapple with legs.

Find the insect that looks like a helmet.

Find the insect that looks like a stick with legs.

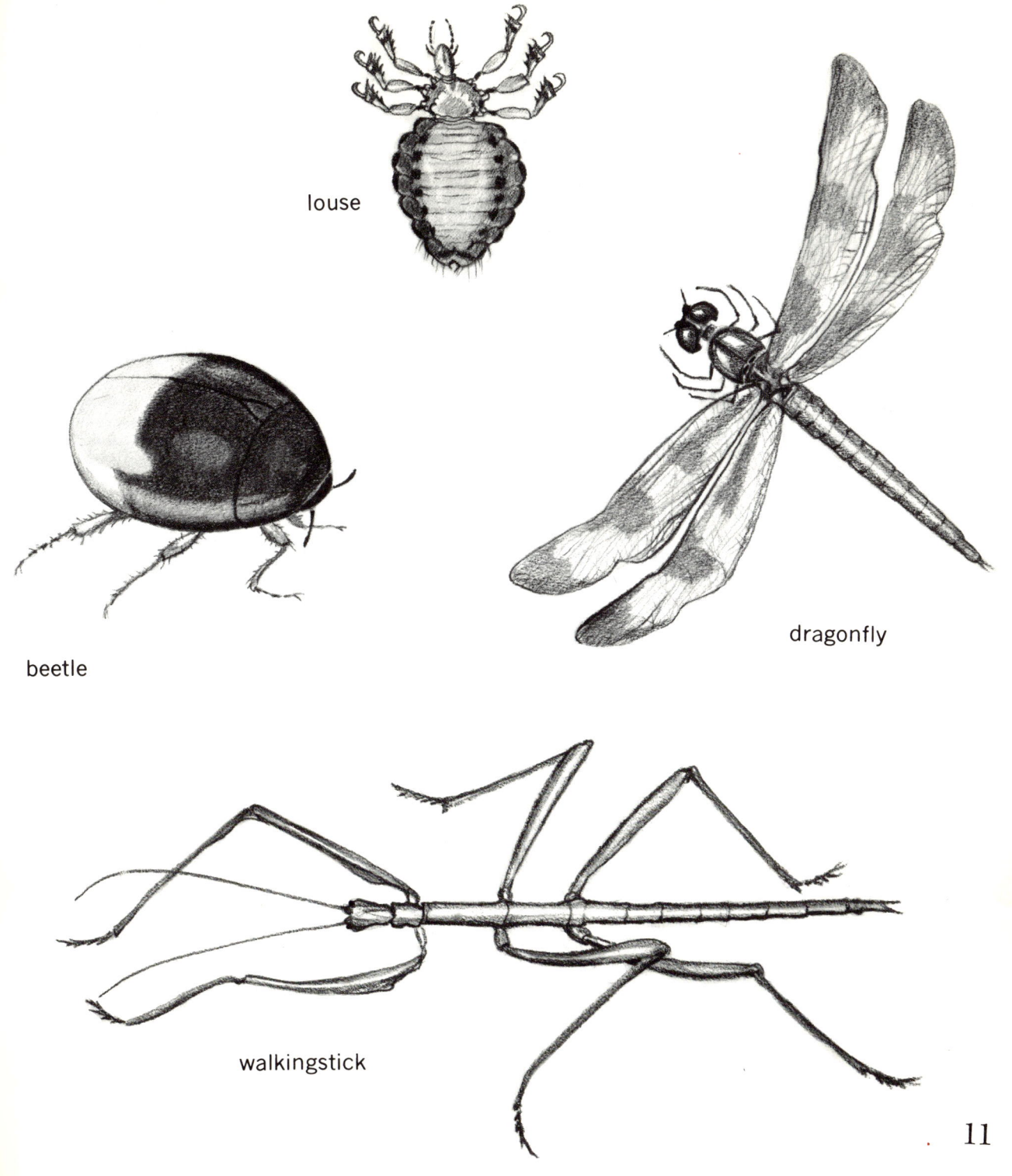

Sometimes you can tell one insect from another by its *antennae*.
The antennae are feelers that stick out of the insect's head.
They help the insect to smell and touch.
Antennae come in many shapes and sizes.

Cave crickets have long antennae.

Leafhoppers have short antennae.

Butterflies have antennae with bumps on the end.

Moths usually have feathered antennae.

Damsel bugs have antennae shaped like elbows.

A puzzle:

Which is which?

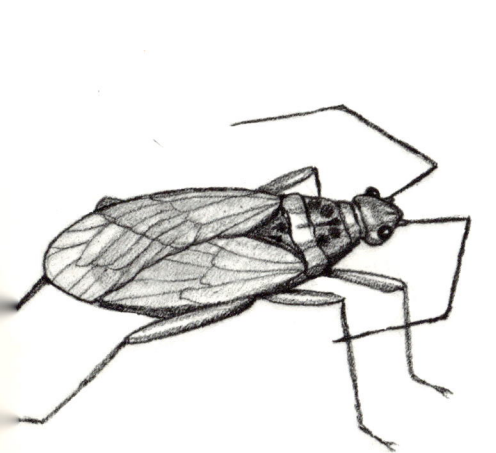
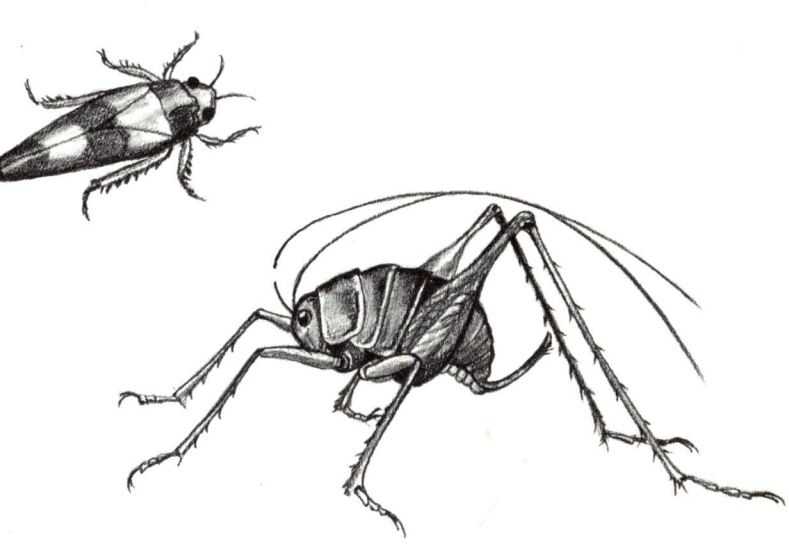

Some insects have strange parts.

Find the insect that seems to have claws on its head.

Find the insect that looks as if its body ends in a pair of ice tongs.

Find the insect that looks as if it has a long nose.

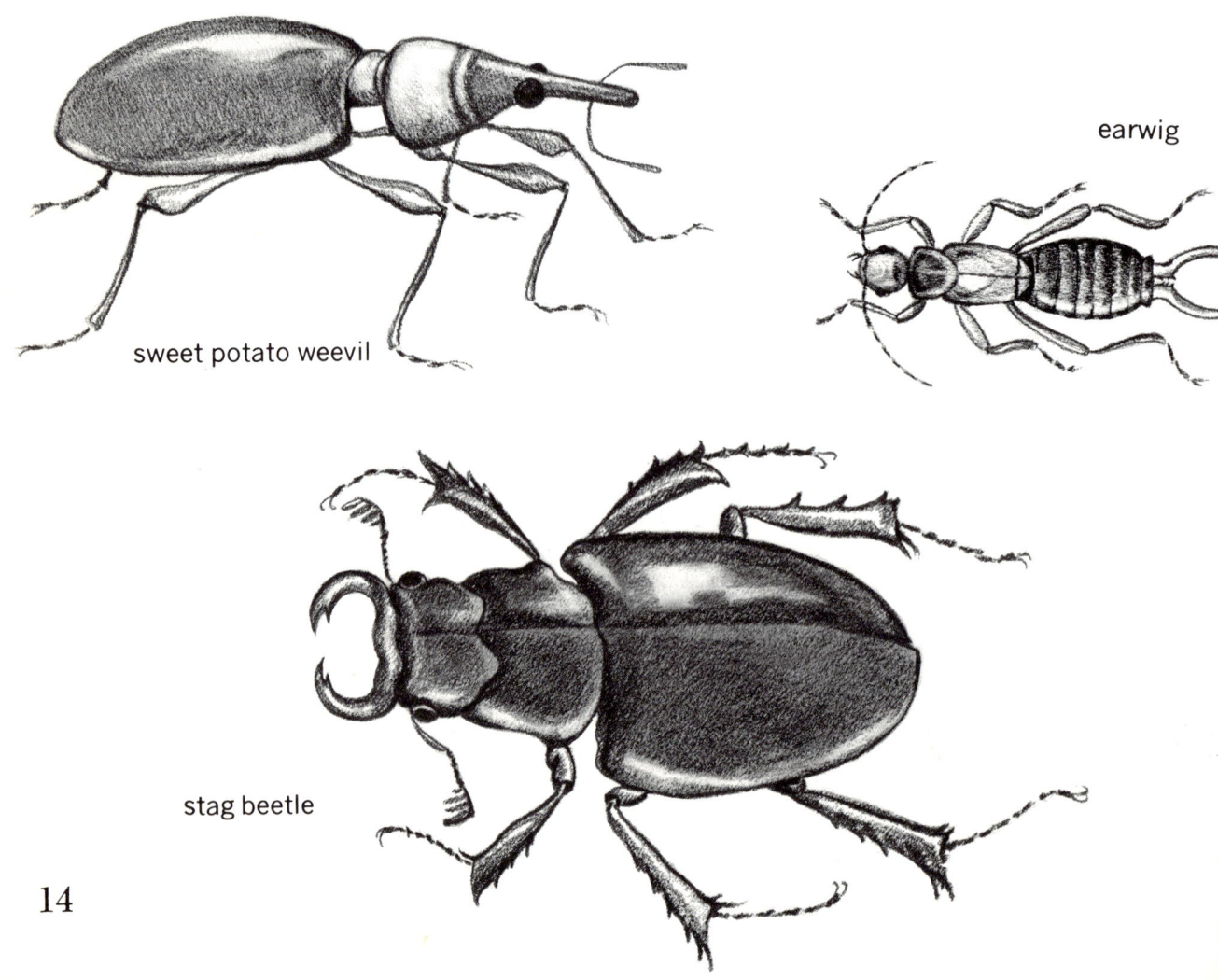

sweet potato weevil

earwig

stag beetle

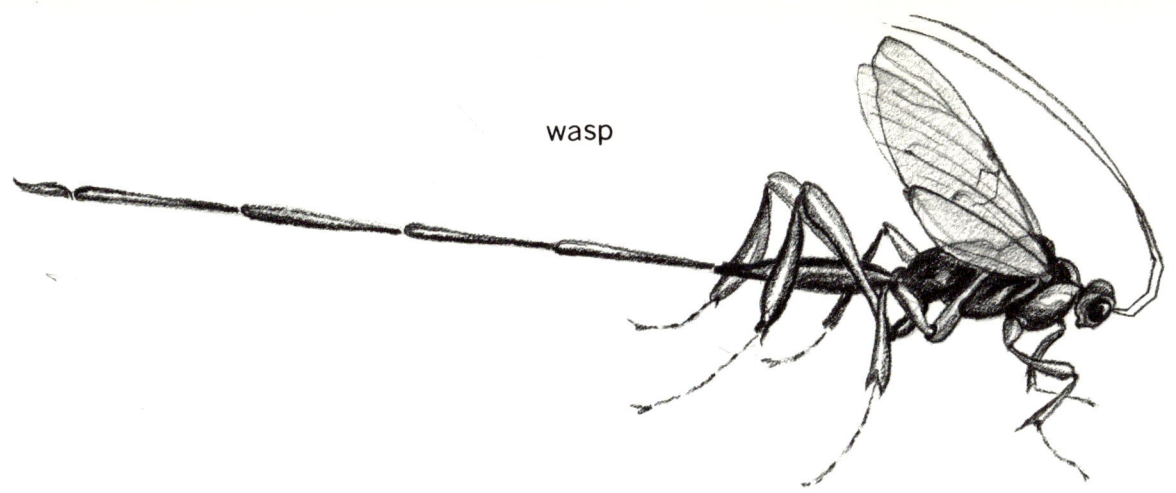
wasp

Find the insect that seems to have threads coming from the end of its body.

Find the insect that ends in the letter "T."

Find the insect that looks as if it has a very long tail.

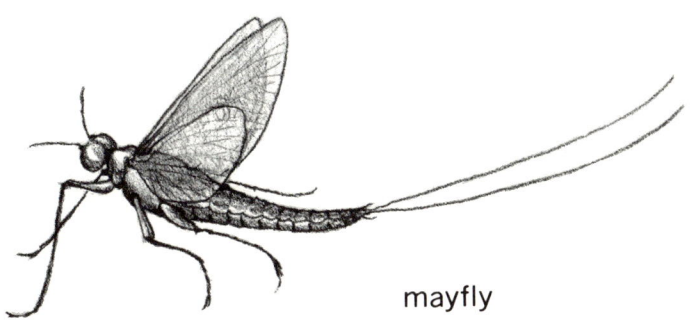
mayfly

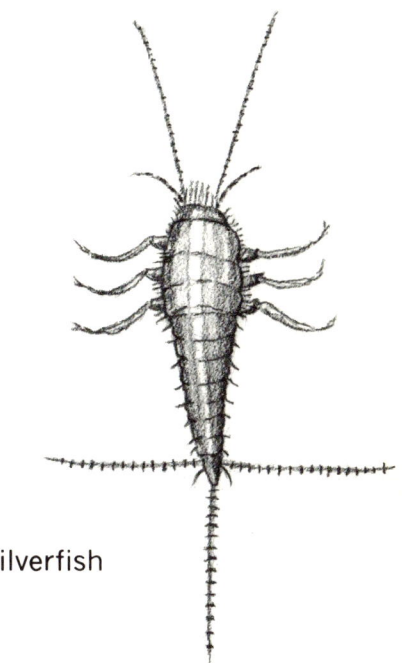
silverfish

The number of wings an insect has can also help you find out what kind it is.
Count the wings on these insects.

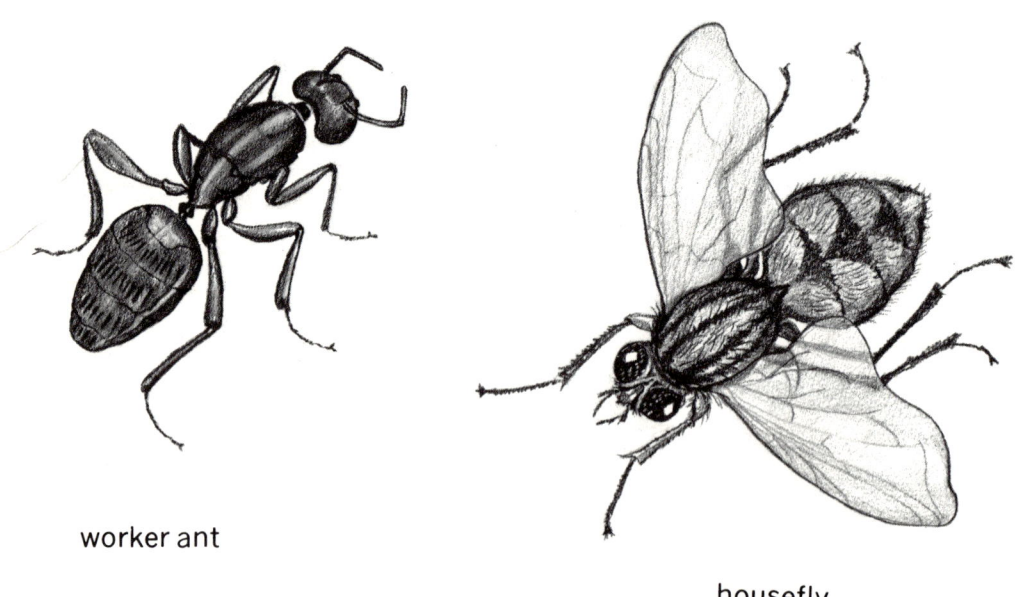

worker ant

housefly

Worker ants have no wings.
Flies have one pair of wings.

But . . .
most insects like moths have two pairs of wings,
a front pair and a hind pair.

luna moth

Sometimes the size of the two pairs of wings helps
to tell insects apart.
The dragonfly has front and hind wings
that are the same size.
The grasshopper's hind wings are larger
than its front wings.
The wasp's hind wings are smaller
than its front wings.

A puzzle:
Here are a dragonfly, a grasshopper, and a wasp with their wings missing.

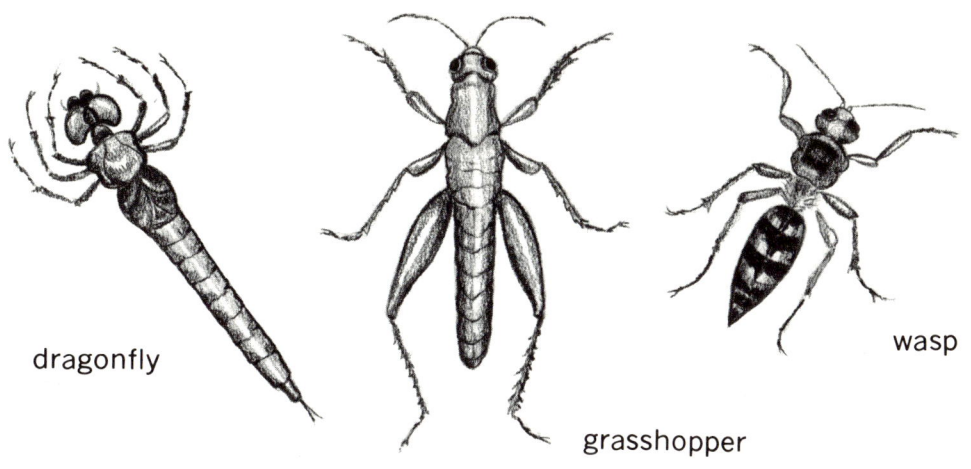

Here are the wings.

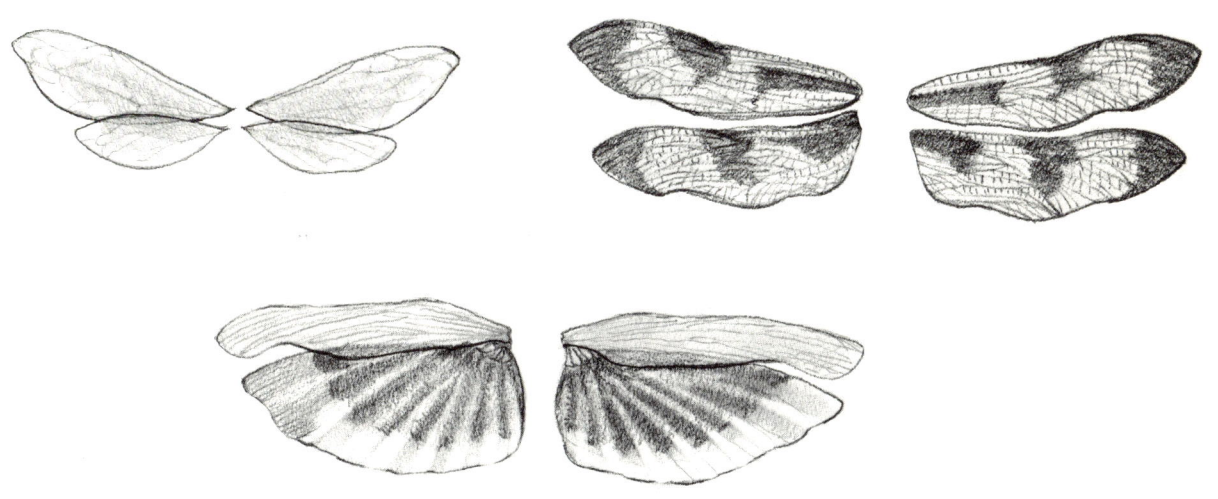

Can you match them to their bodies?

Another way you can tell insects apart is
by the way the wings look and feel.
The lacewings have wings like their name.

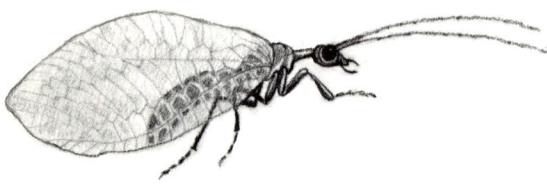

Moths and butterflies have wings with scales.
The scales come off in your hand if you touch the wings.

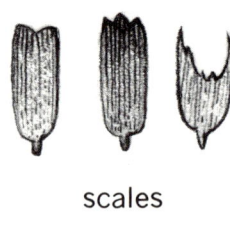

scales

Beetles have tough front wings that cover
much softer hind wings.

front wing

hind wing

Bugs have peculiar front wings.
The front part is hard and tough.
The back part is soft.
Find the hard and soft parts of the
front wings of this bug.

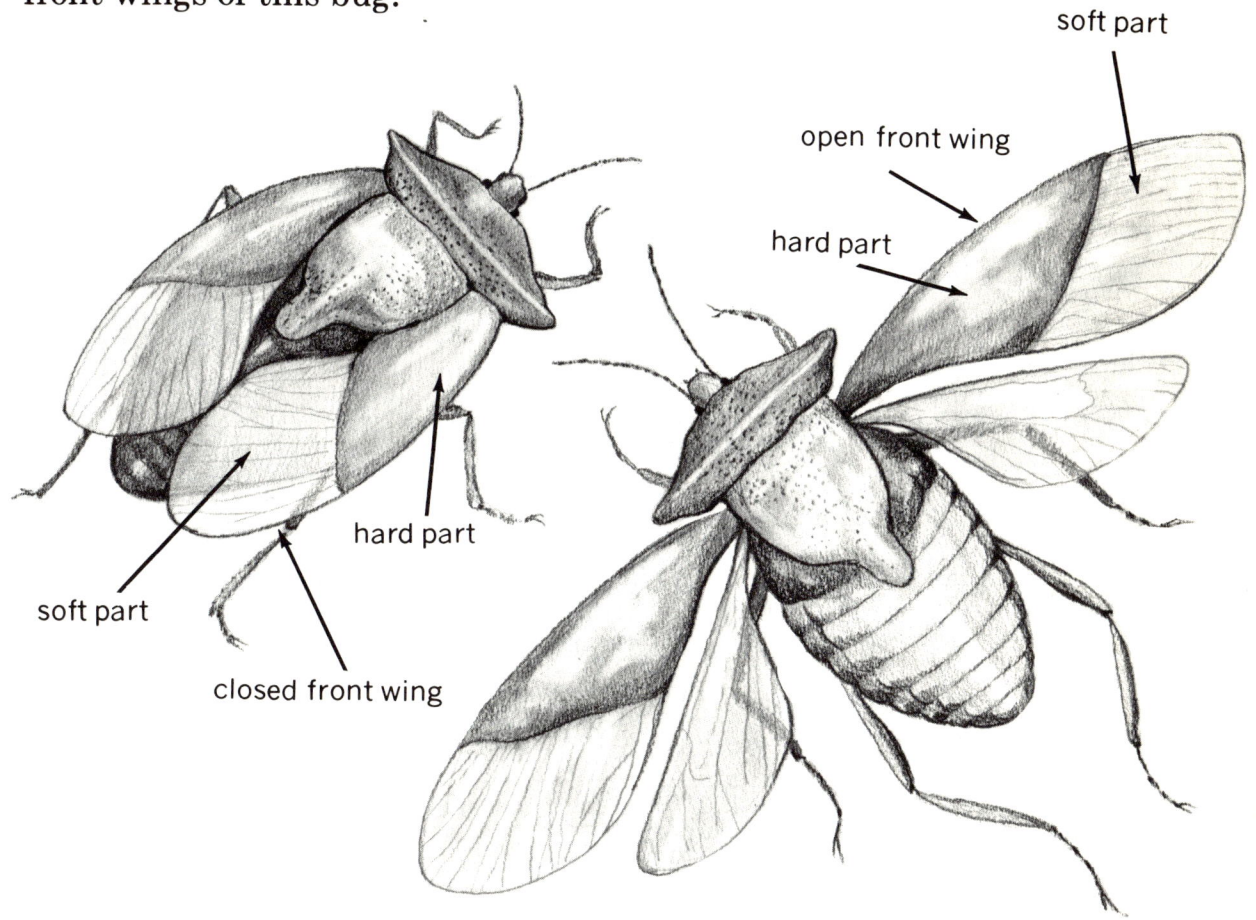

Lots of people call all insects bugs.
But bugs are only one kind of insect.
They are the only insects that have
this special kind of front wing.

21

Insects hold their wings in different ways
when they rest on a branch.
Many butterflies rest with their wings held up over the body.
Many moths rest with their wings held straight out.
Which is which?

Different insects have different kinds of mouths.
The shape of an insect's mouth helps it to eat its special kind of food.

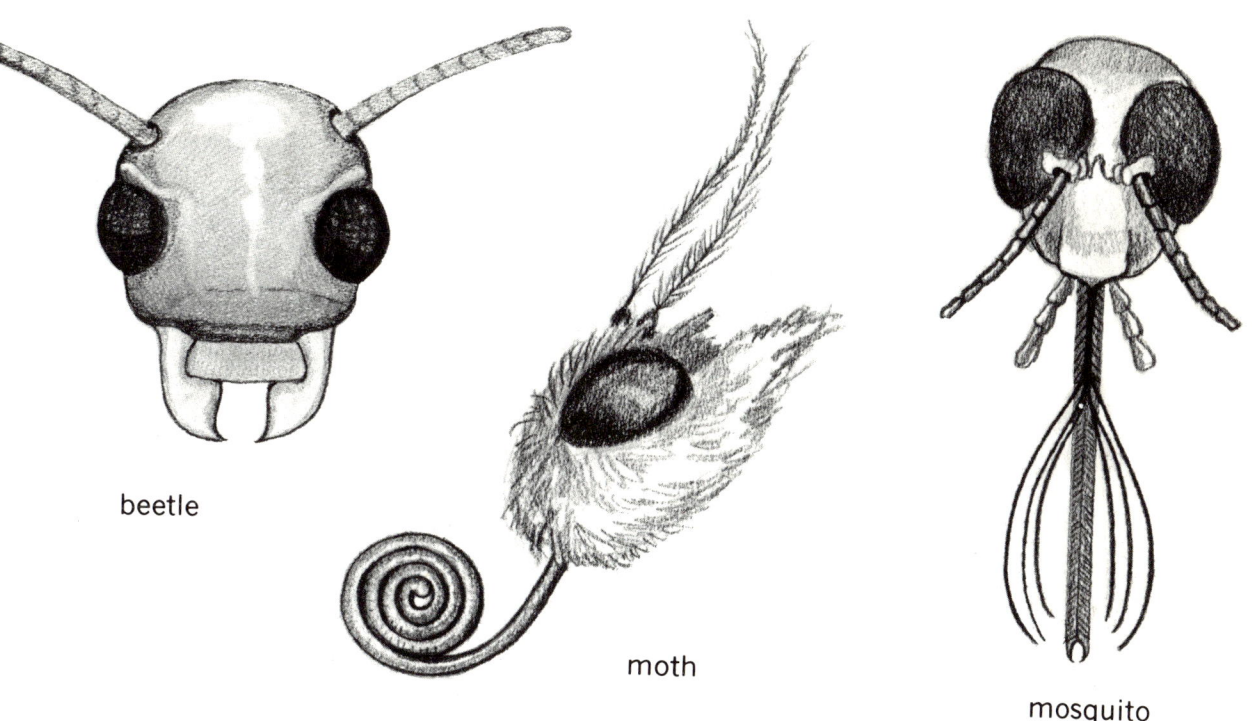

beetle

moth

mosquito

Find the insect that looks as if it has a tongue all rolled up.
When it unrolls, the insect can suck the juice of flowers.

Find the insect that looks as if it can make a hole in your skin and suck your blood.

Find the insect that looks as if its mouth can bite and chew.

When you look at an insect you have to notice many things.

Look at its shape.

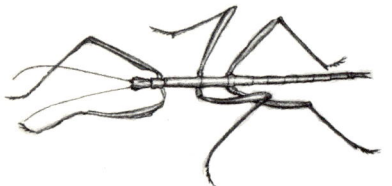  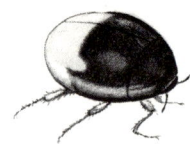 

Look at its antennae.

 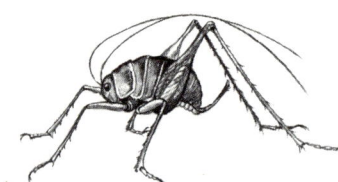 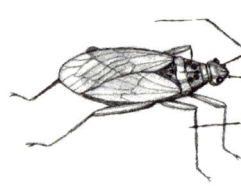 

See if it has any strange parts.

 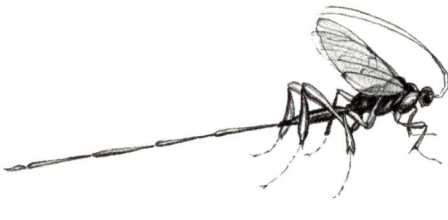 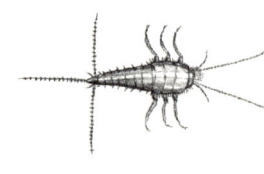

Look at the number of wings and the size of the front and hind wings.

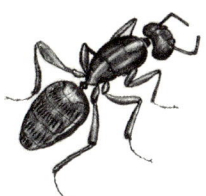  

See whether the wings are hard or soft.

Look at the way the wings are held when the insect is at rest.

The mouth parts are hard to see, but when you catch an insect see if you can tell whether it chews or sucks.

 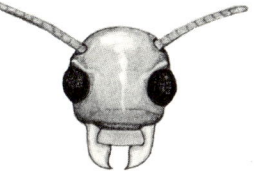

Insects are everywhere.
You can catch them easily.
Use a net to sweep through grass or bushes or use it
to collect moths around an outside light at night.

Put some bait in a glass jar.
It could be a piece of mashed banana, a piece of meat,
or a few drops of molasses.
Then bury the glass jar up to its neck in the ground.

Brush some sweet bait onto the bark of a tree,
a telephone pole, or a fence.
Go back after a while to see what insects
come to feed on it.

Peel the bark from dead trees, and lift up stones,
boards, and logs to see what lives underneath.

Look for dead insects in seaweed along the shore.

Shake bushes above an open umbrella or an old sheet.

Use a strainer to sweep the top of a pond or puddle.

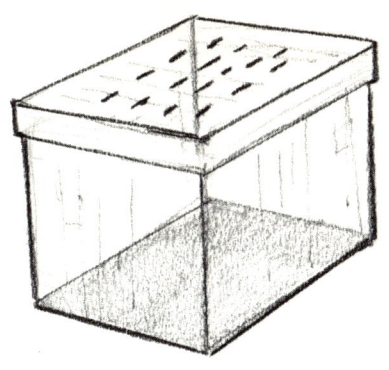

You can use anything for an insect cage:

a *jar*—with a few holes punched in the lid,

a *plastic box*—that also has air holes punched into its cover,

an old *aquarium* or *fish bowl* with a screen or a piece of cheesecloth on top,

any *carton* or *shoebox* with a screen top.

Find out what your insect eats.
Put different kinds of food in its cage.
Insects may eat sugar or fruit,
bread or cereal, and dead or live insects.
They may also eat the leaves of the plant
on which you found them.

How many of these insects do you recognize?

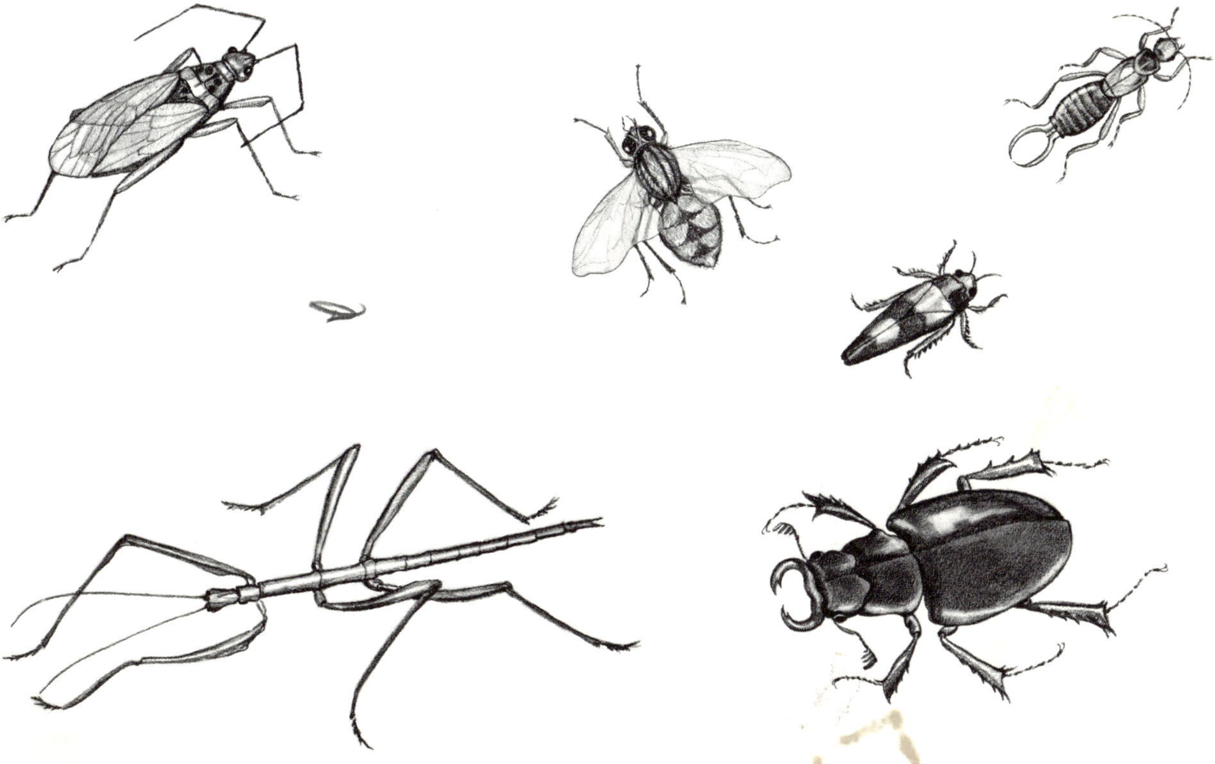

31

ABOUT THE AUTHORS

MILLICENT E. SELSAM, the distinguished author of more than sixty science books for children, majored in biology at Brooklyn College and received her M.A. from Columbia University's Department of Botany. She has taught biology at Brooklyn College and in New York City High Schools.

Mrs. Selsam has received awards for her books from the American Nature Study Society, The Thomas Alva Edison Foundation, and the Boys Club of America.

JOYCE HUNT has a B.A. and an M.A. from Hunter College and teaches primary grades in the New York Public School System. The books of this series are her first published books.

ABOUT THE ARTIST

HARRIETT SPRINGER has a Bachelor of Fine Arts degree from the Carnegie Institute of Technology and has also lived and studied in Mexico. A well-known fabric designer, she often draws on nature's flora and fauna for her unusual creations.